Listening to Others

CIVIC VIRTUES

Marisa Pace

CiViCS FOR THE REAL WORLD™

Rosen Classroom™

Listening to others is important.
It can help you learn.

Look at the person who
is talking.

Sit still in your chair.

Only talk when it is your turn.

Raise your hand if you have questions.

Always be a good listener!

WORDS TO KNOW

chair

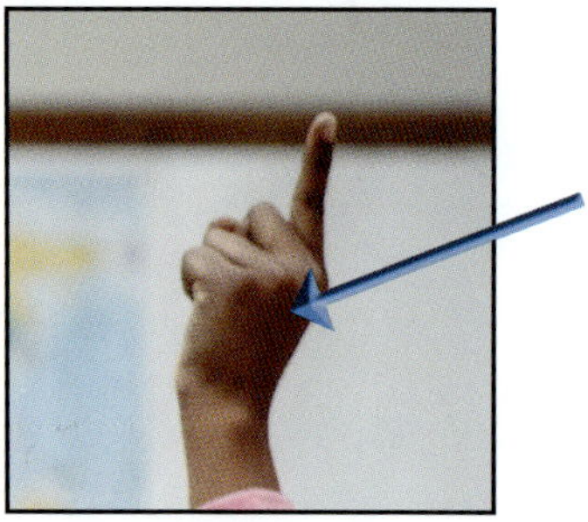

hand